W9-AES-471

Calvin Johnson

By Jeff Savage

AMAZING ATHLETES

 Lerner Publications Company • Minneapolis

For Jaxon Russo—the pride of El Dorado Hills and future football star

Lerner Publications Company
A division of Lerner Publishing Group, Inc.
241 First Avenue North
Minneapolis, MN 55401 U.S.A.

Website address: www.lernerbooks.com

Library of Congress Cataloging-in-Publication Data

Savage, Jeff, 1961–
    Calvin Johnson / by Jeff Savage.
        p.   cm. — (Amazing athletes)
    Includes index.
    ISBN 978–1–4677–0278–2 (lib. bdg. : alk. paper)
    1. Johnson, Calvin, 1985– 2. Football players—United States—Biography—Juvenile literature.
    3. Detroit Lions (Football team)—Juvenile literature. I. Title.
    GV939.J6123S39 2013
    796.332092—dc23 [B]   2012000551

Manufactured in the United States of America
1 – CG – 7/15/12

TABLE OF CONTENTS

Calvin Johnson runs the ball down the field after catching a pass in a 2011 game against the Oakland Raiders.

MEGATRON

Wide receiver Calvin Johnson caught the pass in the middle of the football field. He ran past a **defender**. He shoved another to the ground. Finally, two players tackled him. Calvin was helping his Detroit Lions move down the field once again.

The Lions were playing against the Oakland Raiders in this 2011 National Football League (NFL) game. The Lions had eight wins and five losses on the season. They needed to keep winning to make the **playoffs**.

Detroit was behind, 27–14, with just seven minutes left. Calvin already had one touchdown in the game. Since his touchdown, the Raiders were using two defenders to guard Calvin. This allowed his teammates to get open. The Lions scored a touchdown in just five plays. But they still trailed, 27–21.

Calvin stands 6 feet 5 inches tall and weighs 235 pounds. He is stronger and faster than most of his opponents. Fans and teammates call him Megatron, after the all-powerful robot from the *Transformers* comic books and movies.

The Lions got the football back with two minutes left in the game. They needed to drive 98 yards to win.

Calvin's strength helps him break tackles.

Quarterback Matthew Stafford threw a pass deep to Calvin down the left side of the field. He caught the ball while keeping his toes in bounds. The Lions were up to their own 39-yard line. On the next play, Calvin went deep. Raiders defenders ran with him. Stafford threw a high, wobbly pass. The ball was not thrown far enough. But Calvin changed direction to track the ball. He bent backward and caught it as he fell.

Calvin catches a pass from quarterback Matthew Stafford.

Suddenly the Lions were at the Raiders' 13-yard line. Three plays later, Calvin sprinted down the middle of the field. Stafford fired the pass. Calvin caught it in the back of the **end zone**. Touchdown! The Lions had scored with 39 seconds left. After the **extra point**, Detroit had the lead, 28–27. The Lions won the game!

Calvin catches the game-winning touchdown against the Raiders.

Calvin (left) celebrates the win with teammate Kevin Smith.

Calvin's mother, Arica, says: "Calvin always had a kind nature about him. He was one to pick up opponents off the ground. Sportsmanship was important to him. I always told him, 'If you treat people the way you want to be treated, things will work out.'"

Calvin did not do a fancy dance after scoring. He does not like to brag. Instead, he ran toward his team's side of the field. His teammates swarmed around him. "It's easy to show off if you are making plays all the time. But it's not me," Calvin said. "I have always been like this. I take after my father. I'm just chill. I just lead by example."

Atlanta, Georgia *(above)*, is about 40 miles from Newnan.

RAISED RIGHT

Calvin Johnson was born September 29, 1985, in Newnan, Georgia. Calvin has two sisters and one brother. Calvin's father, also named Calvin, worked as a train **conductor**. Calvin's mother, Arica, worked for the Atlanta public school system. "My parents worked hard and raised us right," Calvin said. School was important. "You didn't want to bring home anything but an A or a B," said Calvin. "To my mom, a C was like an F."

Calvin was always big for his age. But he was not allowed to play tackle football until he reached high school. "My mom thought I would get hurt," he said. Instead, he played Little League baseball. His favorite player was Ken Griffey Jr. In middle school, Calvin was 6 feet tall. By the age of 15, he stood 6 feet 4 inches. In 2000 his mother allowed him to join the football team at Sandy Creek High School in Tyrone, Georgia.

As a child, Calvin was a big fan of Ken Griffey Jr. *(right)*. Griffey played for the Seattle Mariners.

Calvin wore jersey number 81 and played wide receiver. The Sandy Creek Patriots were mainly a running team. They called most of their plays for the **running back**. Even so, Calvin helped his team. He was the Patriots' leading wide receiver. As a junior in 2002, he caught 34 passes and scored 10 touchdowns. His senior year, he caught 40 passes with eight touchdowns.

In 2010, Sandy Creek High School honored Calvin. The school retired Calvin's uniform number 81. No other player on the team will ever wear that jersey number.

Calvin was rated among the nation's top 10 high school receivers. College coaches came to watch him play. Among them was Chan Gailey, the coach at the Georgia Institute of Technology (Georgia Tech). "He was

Chan Gailey coached the Georgia Tech Yellow Jackets from 2002 to 2007.

the biggest, fastest player on the field," said Gailey.

Calvin's football skills and excellent grades allowed him to choose from a long list of colleges. He picked Georgia Tech.

Calvin catches the game-winning touchdown against Clemson University during his freshman year at Georgia Tech.

LIKE SPIDER-MAN

Calvin was an instant star at Georgia Tech. In his first game as a freshman in 2004, he caught eight passes for 127 yards to help his Yellow Jackets beat Samford University.

At the end of a game against North Carolina State University, the Yellow Jackets were driving for the winning score. A pass over the middle was thrown behind Calvin. He reached back and squeezed it with his big right hand. "He pulled it in like Spider-Man," said defender Marcus Hudson. ESPN rated the catch the second-best play of the college football season.

"He's so talented, but he also outworks a lot of our older kids," said Georgia Tech assistant coach Buddy Geis. In the 2004 Champs Sports Bowl against Syracuse University, Calvin made a diving catch for Georgia Tech's first touchdown. The Yellow Jackets won, 51–14.

Calvin trained even harder for his second year at Georgia Tech. "As long as I improve on last

Calvin beats a University of Georgia defender for a touchdown in 2005.

season's performance I will be satisfied," he said. He opened the 2005 season with a 35-yard touchdown catch at Auburn University. Calvin became the first Georgia Tech player in five years to be named first-team all-American.

Calvin studied building construction at Georgia Tech. He worked during the summer to earn college credit. He had two choices. He could help build fancy homes in Georgia. Or he could travel to the South American country of Bolivia to help build restrooms for people in need. Calvin chose to go to Bolivia.

Calvin returned to Georgia Tech in 2006 for his junior year. He was unstoppable. He scored touchdowns of 58 and 66 yards on back-to-back plays against the University of Virginia. One week later, he caught two more touchdowns against Virginia Tech University.

Calvin catches a touchdown with defenders all around him at the Gator Bowl.

Calvin finished the 2006 season at the Gator Bowl with two more touchdowns. He won the Fred Biletnikoff Award as college football's best wide receiver. In three years at Georgia Tech, Calvin shattered school records for career yards and touchdowns. He announced that he was skipping his senior season to join the NFL.

Calvin holds his new Detroit Lions jersey.

LEARNING TO FIGHT

A wide receiver is rarely the first pick in the NFL **draft**. The Oakland Raiders held the top pick and selected quarterback JaMarcus Russell. The Detroit Lions picked next. They took Calvin.

Calvin signed a six-year **contract** worth $64 million, making him the highest-paid player in Lions history. He was rich. But he cared more about helping Detroit win. Calvin met with Lions **general manager** Matt Millen in his office. Millen once was a fierce defender. "If I lined up over you," Millen asked Calvin, "how are you going to get past me?" Calvin replied: "With all due respect, sir, I would run right by you."

Calvin impressed his new teammates and coaches with his strength and speed. Fellow wide receiver Roy Williams quickly gave him the nickname Megatron.

Teammate Roy Williams *(right)* gave Calvin the nickname Megatron in 2007.

In Calvin's first game as a **rookie** in 2007, he caught four passes for 70 yards and a touchdown.

In 2008, the Lions traded Williams. Calvin became the team's top wide receiver. But he had little help from his teammates. The Lions became the first team in league history to lose all 16 of their games. Calvin led the NFL with 12 touchdowns, but few people noticed. He wasn't even voted to the **Pro Bowl**.

Calvin's second season in Detroit was difficult. The team lost all of their games.

In 2009, the Lions selected quarterback Matthew Stafford with the first pick in the draft. With Stafford throwing to Calvin, the Lions would be harder to stop. Calvin used his strength to run over defenders. New York Jets defender Darrelle Revis said: "Calvin Johnson is a beast. He should be illegal." But Stafford suffered several injuries. The team finished 2–14.

Opponents guarded Calvin with two defenders in 2010. Stafford didn't care. He often forced passes to Calvin even if he

Quarterback Matthew Stafford helped the Lions improve in 2010.

Calvin's skills are often tested against two defenders.

was covered. Stafford knew that Calvin could not be stopped by even two defenders.

The Lions started the 2010 season with two wins and 10 losses. Then they got hot. They won their last four games. Detroit was improving. Calvin led the Lions in receiving for the third year in a row. He finally was selected to the Pro Bowl.

Calvin makes a leaping catch during a game against the Dallas Cowboys in 2011.

ALWAYS WORK HARD

The Lions became winners in 2011. In the third game of the season, Detroit trailed the Minnesota Vikings, 20–0, at halftime. Calvin helped bring his team back with two touchdowns. On one catch, he lowered his shoulder and drove a defender into the turf.

In overtime against the Vikings, Calvin caught a pass over his shoulder with his fingertips while falling to the ground. On the next play, Jason Hanson kicked a **field goal** to win the game, 26–23.

The next week, Detroit fell behind the Dallas Cowboys, 30–17. Then Calvin caught a touchdown pass early in the fourth quarter. Later, Calvin burned defender Terence Newman for another touchdown with 1:39 left to win the game, 34–30.

Calvin makes the winning catch for a 34–30 victory over the Cowboys.

Calvin caught two touchdowns in each of his team's first four games in 2011 to set an NFL record. The Lions started the season 5–0. Their record climbed to 9–5 with their win at Oakland. They needed one more victory to reach the playoffs. The high-powered San

The Lions celebrate reaching the playoffs after defeating the Chargers.

Diego Chargers came to Ford Field in Detroit. The Lions crushed them, 38–10.

The Lions faced star quarterback Drew Brees and the New Orleans Saints in the first round of the playoffs. Calvin caught a touchdown in the second quarter to give Detroit the lead, 14–7. But Brees and the Saints ran away with the game from there, winning 45–28.

Former Detroit Lions general manager Matt Millen said: "Calvin has great character. He makes great decisions. He owns up to mistakes. He is everything you could ever want in a player, a teammate, and a son."

Two of Calvin's fans cheer him on during a game in 2011.

Calvin is considered the best wide receiver in the NFL. He could be great for many years. "This kid is as humble as you can be," says Lions receivers coach Shawn Jefferson. "But Sunday at 1 o'clock, you better be ready, because he is coming at you like a freight train."

Calvin says practice is the key to success. "Always work hard," he says. "Never stop until the coach makes you."

Calvin signs a ball for a fan at training camp in 2011.

Selected Career Highlights

2011   Named NFL first-team All-Pro for the first time
Led the Lions with 96 receptions, 1,681 yards receiving, and 16 touchdowns
Selected to the Pro Bowl for the second time
Became the first player in NFL history with two touchdown receptions in each of a team's first four games of the season

2010   Named NFL second-team All-Pro for the first time
Selected to the Pro Bowl for the first time
Led the Lions with 77 receptions, 1,120 yards receiving, and 12 touchdowns
Tied career high with 10 receptions against the Buffalo Bills
Tied career high with 10 receptions against the Tampa Bay Buccaneers

2009   Led the Lions with 67 receptions and 984 yards receiving

2008   Led the NFL in touchdown receptions (12)
Led the Lions with 78 receptions
Scored a career-long 96-yard touchdown against the Houston Texans

2007   Was the second-overall choice in the NFL draft by the Detroit Lions
Became the highest-paid player in Lions history
Scored a touchdown in his first NFL game

2006   Led Georgia Tech with 76 receptions, 1,202 yards, and 15 touchdowns
Set the school record for receiving touchdowns in a season
Received the Fred Biletnikoff Award as the nation's top receiver
Named first-team All-American

2005   Led Georgia Tech with 54 receptions, 888 yards, and six touchdowns
Named first-team All-American, the first Georgia Tech player in five years so honored

2004   Led Georgia Tech with 48 receptions, 837 yards, and seven touchdowns
Named first-team All Atlantic Coast Conference (ACC)
Named ACC Rookie of the Year.

2003   Led Sandy Creek High School with 40 receptions and eight touchdowns
Named first-team All-State

2002   Led Sandy Creek High School with 34 receptions and 10 touchdowns

Glossary

conductor: a person in charge of a train

contract: a deal signed by a player and a team that states the amount of money the player is paid and the number of years he plays

defender: a football player whose job it is to stop the other team from scoring points

draft: a yearly event in which professional teams take turns choosing new players from a selected group

end zone: the area beyond the goal line at each end of the football field. A team scores six points when it reaches the other team's end zone.

extra point: a successful kick over the crossbar and between the two upright poles after a touchdown. An extra point is worth one point.

field goal: a successful kick over the crossbar and between the two upright poles. A field goal is worth three points.

general manager: the person who makes decisions about players for a sports team

playoffs: a series of games held every year to decide a champion

Pro Bowl: a game played at the end of the season featuring the top players in the American Football Conference and the National Football Conference

quarterback: a football player whose main job is to throw passes

rookie: a first-year player

running back: a football player whose main job is to run with the ball

wide receiver: a football player whose main job is to catch passes

Further Reading & Websites

Kennedy, Mike, and Mark Stewart. *Touchdown: The Power and Precision of Football's Perfect Play*. Minneapolis: Millbrook Press, 2010.

Savage, Jeff. *Drew Brees*. Minneapolis: Lerner Publications Company, 2011.

Sports Illustrated Kids 1st and 10: Top 10 Lists of Everything in Football. New York: Time Home Entertainment, 2011.

Detroit Lions: The Official Site
http://www.nfl.com/lions
The official website of the Detroit Lions that includes the team schedule and game results, late-breaking news, team history, biographies of players like Calvin Johnson, and much more.

Georgia Institute of Technology Sports: The Official Site
http://www.ramblinwreck.com
The official home of the Georgia Tech sports programs that features game results, biographies of current and former players like Calvin Johnson, all-time records, and more.

The Official Site of the National Football League
http://www.nfl.com
The NFL's official website provides fans with the latest scores, schedules, and standings; biographies and statistics of players; and the league's official online store.

Sports Illustrated Kids
http://www.sikids.com
The *Sports Illustrated Kids* website covers all sports, including the NFL.

Index

Photo Acknowledgments

The images in this book are used with the permission of: © Leon Halip/Getty Images, pp. 4, 28, 29; © Thearon W. Henderson/Getty Images, p. 6; © Kirby Lee/US Presswire, p. 7; © Jason O. Watson/US Presswire, p. 8; AP Photo/Paul Sakuma, p. 9; © Andrew Gunners/Digital Vision/Getty Images, p. 10; © Focus on Sport/Getty Images, p. 11; Sean Meyers/Icon SMI717/Sean Meyers Photography/Newscom, p. 13; © Grant Halverson/Stringer/Getty Images, p. 14; © Christopher Gooley/US Presswire, p. 16; © Marc Serota/Stringer/Getty Images, p. 18; © Justin Kase Conder/US Presswire, p. 19; © Geoff Burke/US Presswire, p. 20; © Gregory Shamus/Stringer/Getty Images, p. 21; © Scott Cunningham/Getty Images, pp. 22, 23; © Matthew Emmons/US Presswire, p. 24; © Tim Heitman/US Presswire, p. 25; MSA/Icon SMI CAD/Newscom, p. 26; AP Photo/Duane Burleson, p. 27.

Front cover: AP Photo/Carlos Osorio.

Main body text set in Caecilia LT Std 16/28.
Typeface provided by Adobe Systems.